An Encyclopedia of

TUDOR MEDICINE

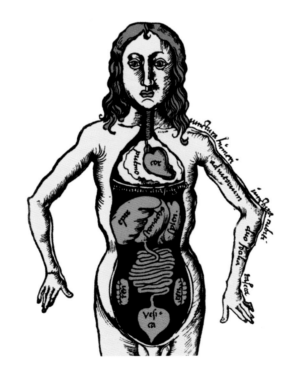

Jane Penrose

How to use this encyclopedia

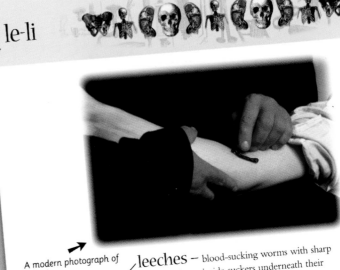

le-li

A modern photograph of a leech.

These combs for removing nits were found on the Mary Rose.

leeches – blood-sucking worms with sharp teeth which are inside suckers underneath their bodies. The leeches' teeth can bite through skin, so they were used for *blood-letting*. This was not painful, because leeches produce slime that works as an *anaesthetic*. (see BLOOD-LETTING)

lice – insects that live in hair and on skin. Tudor people often had lice because they lived close to animals, and lice were passed from animals to humans. Combs with very sharp points were used to comb lice out of the hair. If this did not work the hair was cut off.

Page headings

Encyclopedias work in alphabetical order. You can tell which letters are on which pages by looking at the page headings. They show the first two letters of the first and last entries on each page.

Headwords

The headwords are the words being described in the encyclopedia. These are in **bold** type.

Abbreviations

The following abbreviations are used:

e.g.	=	for example
etc.	=	et cetera

mortar – bowl in which *herbs* were crushed for medicine. A *pestle* was used to grind herbs in the mortar. Mortars are still used today for preparing herbs and spices in cooking. (see PESTLE)

nits – common name for lice. (see LICE)

operation – cutting open a body to cure or remove a diseased part. Tudor doctors did operations, but did not know enough about the human body to do them safely. There were no *anaesthetics* so operations were extremely painful. *Amputation* was the most common operation.

Paré, Ambroise (1509-1590) – *barber-surgeon* for the French army. He thought the way other doctors did *surgery* was cruel and painful. So instead of using red-hot pokers to stop bleeding, Paré used *salves*, which were more effective and less painful. Paré also discovered a kind of *anaesthetic*. Before *amputation* he tied tight cords above and below where he was going to cut. This stopped the blood and made it far less painful for the patient.

15

Cross-references

Difficult words used in the explanations may be explained somewhere else in the encyclopedia. If this is the case, the difficult word will be in *italic* type. You can look it up to find out what it means.

Sometimes one explanation will be on the same subject as another explanation somewhere else in the encyclopedia. If this is the case, you will find a cross-reference in SMALL CAPITALS at the end of the explanation. You can look up the word in SMALL CAPITALS to find out more about that subject.

People and dates

If the headword is a person's name, their surname is given first. The dates that person was alive are given in brackets.

3

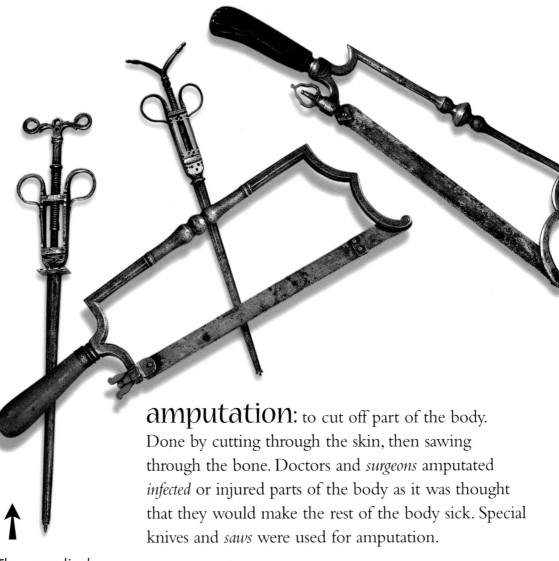

These medical instruments were found on the Tudor ship, the *Mary Rose*. The saws are for amputation.

amputation: to cut off part of the body. Done by cutting through the skin, then sawing through the bone. Doctors and *surgeons* amputated *infected* or injured parts of the body as it was thought that they would make the rest of the body sick. Special knives and *saws* were used for amputation.

anaesthetic: given to patients to stop them feeling pain. Little was known about anaesthetics in Tudor times, so *surgery* was often very painful for the patient. Usually the patient would be made drunk, or punched, to make them unconscious so that they would not feel pain.

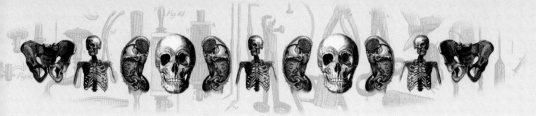

anatomy: scientific name for the human body. Many Tudor doctors studied anatomy, to discover how the human body worked. (see VESALIUS and PARÉ)

apothecary: person who made medicines and sold them in a shop, similar to a modern-day chemist. People went to apothecaries because they were much cheaper than doctors.

This 16th century drawing shows the Tudor view of anatomy. It shows how much Tudor doctors knew about the human body. ⬅

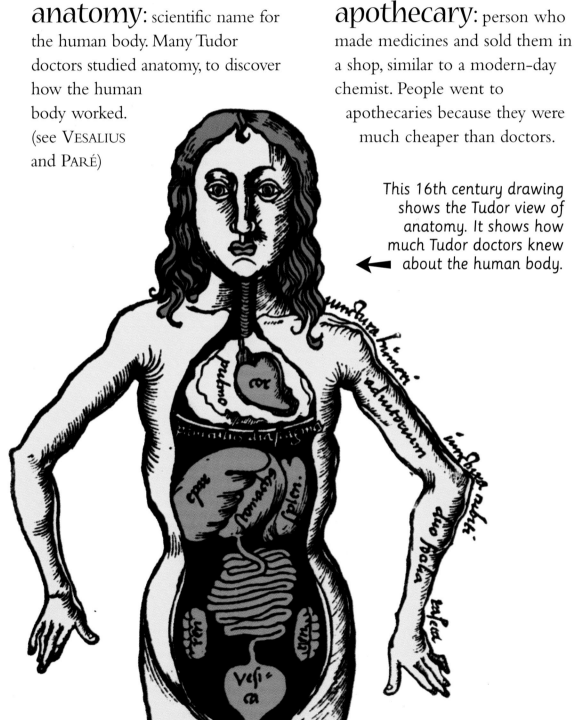

5

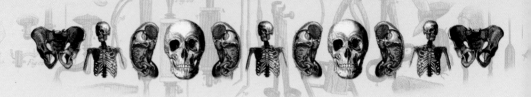

Serratura.

A barber-surgeon performing an amputation in the 16th century. The patient's eyes have been covered so he cannot look at what the barber-surgeon is doing. He may have been knocked out to stop him feeling pain.

barber-surgeon:

person who cut hair, and performed *operations*. Barber-surgeons *amputated* legs and arms, pulled out teeth and stitched cuts. They did not always use clean medical *instruments* and so spread *infection*. They had no *anaesthetics*, so *surgery* was very painful for their patients.

bile: bitter greeny-brown

liquid. Tudor doctors believed there were two kinds of bile – black and yellow – and that they were two *humours*. They believed that too much bile in your body would make you ill. Modern doctors know that bile occurs in the liver and helps bodies to use food. (see HUMOURS)

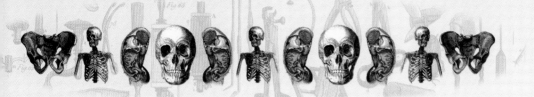

blood-letting:

cutting the skin to let out blood. Tudor people thought that blood was a *humour* and too much blood would make you ill. People who were unwell went to doctors to get rid of some blood. Doctors made careful cuts in the skin, and let them bleed. Sometimes a *leech* was put on the skin to suck the patient's blood. (see HUMOURS and LEECHES)

burn: skin injury caused

by touching something hot. Tudor doctors treated burns by trying to cool the skin. *Salves* or snails were put on the skin. Snails leave a cold trail of slime when they move which cools skin. Some modern doctors use snails to treat burned skin.

de gresse que les braceletz de sa femme luy seruoient, d'an= neaux a ses doigtz, comme les historiens escriuent. Comme

en semblable ce grand tirant Denis Heraclet se laissa si- bien transporter a ses delices qu'il s'habitua en fin de ne faire

A page from a Tudor book showing blood-letting using leeches.

7

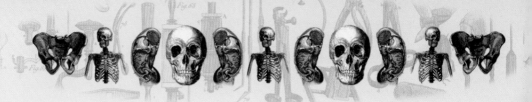

chest: wooden box where doctors kept *instruments* and medicines. Inside were glass bottles for medicines and cures, and instruments for *operating* on patients.

This medical chest was found on the *Mary Rose*, a ship that sank in 1545 and was raised in 1982. You can see the glass bottles that were used for storing medicines.

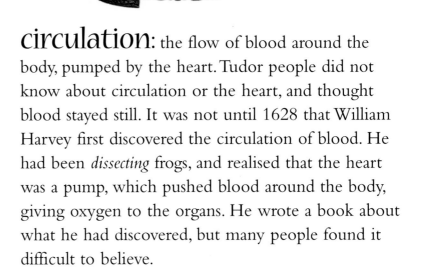

circulation: the flow of blood around the body, pumped by the heart. Tudor people did not know about circulation or the heart, and thought blood stayed still. It was not until 1628 that William Harvey first discovered the circulation of blood. He had been *dissecting* frogs, and realised that the heart was a pump, which pushed blood around the body, giving oxygen to the organs. He wrote a book about what he had discovered, but many people found it difficult to believe.

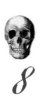

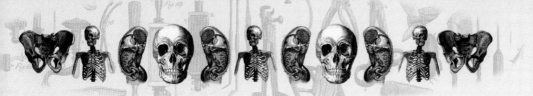
dentist: person who looks after teeth. Tudor dentists did not know that *toothache* was caused by dirty teeth. They thought it was caused by tiny worms inside the tooth. To get rid of the worms, the patient had to put a bowl of water under his chin, then hold a burning candle inside his mouth. The worms would become sleepy from the smell of the candle, drop out into the bowl of water and drown. If the tooth still ached, the dentist would pull it out. This was done using an *extractor*, like a big pair of pliers. There was no *anaesthetic*, so it was very painful.

dissection: cutting up dead animals or humans to discover how their bodies work. Done by doctors and *surgeons* to help them learn about the body and how to treat it. Before Tudor times human dissection was illegal. People who wanted to dissect humans had to steal bodies from graves. In 1565 Queen Elizabeth I said that it was legal for practising surgeons to dissect humans.
(see VESALIUS)

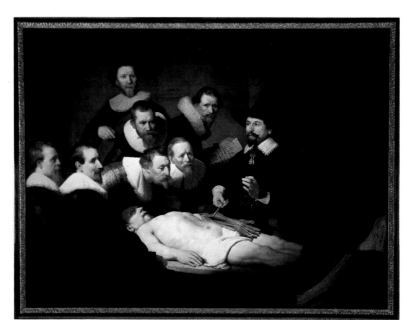

A dissection being performed by a teacher, to train his students about the human body. This is a very famous picture, painted by Rembrandt in 1632.

9

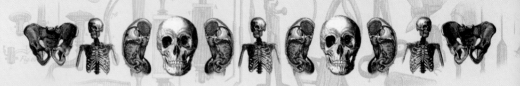

← These dental instruments look like those used in Tudor times. Similar instruments are still used today.

extractor: *instrument* used to pull out teeth. (see DENTIST)

fever: over-heating of the body caused by illness. Tudor people thought that fever was caused by having too much blood, as blood was the *humour* that made heat. They tried to cure this by *blood-letting*. (see HUMOURS and BLOOD-LETTING)

germs: tiny invisible organisms that live in food, dirt or the body. Tudor doctors thought most illnesses were caused by having too much of one *humour*. In fact, most illnesses are caused by germs being in the body. Germs enter the body when people eat bad food, are *unhygienic* or have contact with an ill person.

gout: illness that causes toes and feet to swell painfully. Tudor doctors thought gout was cured by rubbing frogs' legs on the patient's feet. Another cure was to boil a dog, then mix its flesh with worms, fat and *herbs* and rub the mixture on the gout.

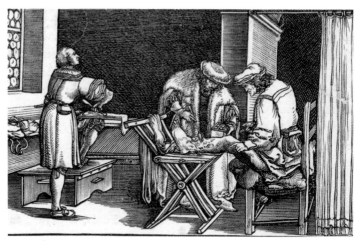

↑ This patient has gout. You can see how swollen his leg and foot are.

A Tudor drawing of a herb garden. The man wearing the hat is a physician. ↑

herbs: plants grown to use in food or medicine. Most Tudor houses had herb gardens and Tudor doctors used herbs in many medicines. They knew a great deal about herbs, and what they cured. Some Tudor herbal cures are still used today, like feverfew to get rid of headaches.

11

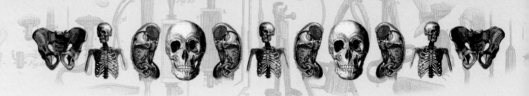

hospital: place where ill or wounded people go to get better. Doctors and nurses work in hospitals. Tudor hospitals were not as *hygienic* as modern hospitals. They were often in cold buildings, with dirty beds and many *germs*. People who went to hospital to get better sometimes came out worse.

humours: the four liquids that Tudors thought made up the human body: blood, black *bile*, yellow *bile* and *phlegm*. It was thought that too much of one humour caused illness. To be cured you had to reduce that humour, e.g. too much blood was treated by *blood-letting*.

The four humours and the effects Tudor people thought they had.

blood	black bile	yellow bile	phlegm
too much blood made you hot and feverish	*too much black bile made you sad and miserable*	*too much yellow bile made you angry and quick-tempered*	*too much phlegm made you cold and tired*

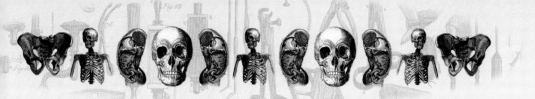
hygiene: cleanliness. Lack of hygiene spreads *germs*. Tudor people did not worry as much about hygiene as we do now. They did not wash often because soap was expensive. Queen Elizabeth I took one bath a month.

infection: to get a disease because of *germs*. *Hygiene* reduces chances of infection. Tudor people often got infections, especially if they had cuts or sores, because germs could get under the skin.

instruments: special tools used by doctors and *surgeons*, e.g. *saw*, *scalpel*, etc.

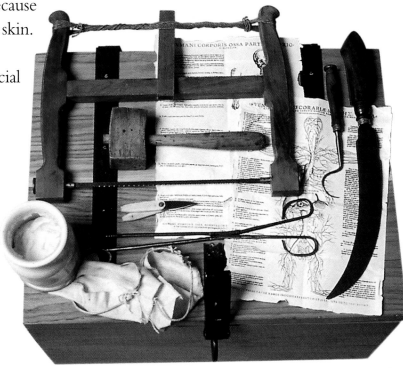

Tudor instruments ➡ used in surgery. The saw and scalpel were for amputation, and the pot was for storing salves.

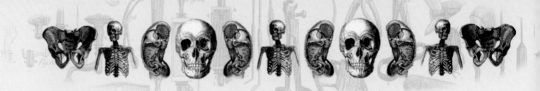

A modern photograph of a leech.

These combs for removing nits were found on the *Mary Rose*.

leeches: blood-sucking worms with sharp teeth which are inside suckers underneath their bodies. The leeches' teeth can bite through skin, so they were used for *blood-letting*. This was not painful, because leeches produce slime that works as an *anaesthetic*. (see BLOOD–LETTING)

lice: insects that live in hair and on skin. Tudor people often had lice because they lived close to animals, and lice were passed from animals to humans. Combs with very sharp points were used to comb lice out of the hair. If this did not work the hair was cut off.

mortar: bowl in which *herbs* were crushed for medicine. A *pestle* was used to grind herbs in the mortar. Mortars are still used today for preparing herbs and spices in cooking. (see PESTLE)

nits: common name for lice. (see LICE)

operation: cutting open a body to cure or remove a diseased part. Tudor doctors did operations, but did not know enough about the human body to do them safely. There were no *anaesthetics* so operations were extremely painful. *Amputation* was the most common operation.

Paré, Ambroise (1509-1590): *barber-surgeon* for the French army. He thought the way other doctors did *surgery* was cruel and painful. So instead of using red-hot pokers to stop bleeding, Paré used *salves*, which were more effective and less painful. Paré also discovered a kind of *anaesthetic*. Before *amputation* he tied tight cords above and below where he was going to cut. This stopped the blood and made it far less painful for the patient.

← This 16th century man is mixing medicines with a pestle and mortar.

pestle: tool with round end, used to crush *herbs* in a *mortar*. (see MORTAR)

phlegm: thick slime in the nose or throat especially during a cold. Tudor doctors thought phlegm was a *humour*. People with too much phlegm were made to drink milk, because doctors thought milk would reduce phlegm. We now know that it does the opposite – it increases phlegm. (see HUMOURS)

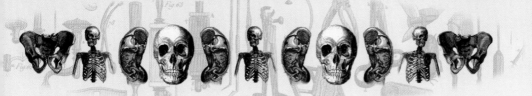

physician: doctor who gave out medicines but did not examine patients. Tudor physicians rarely did *surgery* and knew little about it. There were about a thousand physicians in England in Tudor times.

poultice: heated wet mixture of *herbs* and other ingredients, placed on the body as a cure. Tudor doctors used poultices for bruises, cuts, spots, etc. The heat in the poultice relieved soreness and swelling. Some worked and are still used today, e.g. a poultice of bread and milk on an in-growing toenail.

↑ A Tudor physician at work. His two helpers are fetching and mixing medicines. A customer is showing the physician a list of what he needs.

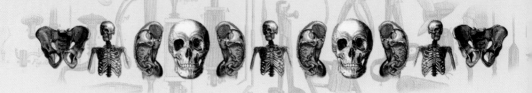

quack: Tudor nickname for a doctor. Some Tudor doctors wore masks filled with *herbs* over their mouths to avoid catching *germs* from their patients. The masks looked like beaks so doctors were called quacks as a joke. We still use the nickname today.

Renaissance: period between 14th and 16th centuries when many new scientific discoveries were made in Europe. Art improved too, with painters like Leonardo da Vinci painting accurate pictures of human and animal *anatomy*. Medicine improved because people started to understand the human body better. Human *dissection* was made legal for some people. This helped in art and medicine.

A drawing of a baby in the womb, by Leonardo da Vinci. Leonardo is one of the most famous Renaissance artists. He studied anatomy and performed dissection to learn more about the human body.

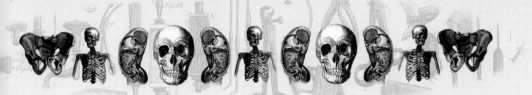

salve: soothing cream or grease used as a cure. Salves were made by crushing *herbs* using a *pestle* and *mortar*, then mixing with oils and fat. Tudor doctors made salves to sooth bruised, *burned*, or cut skin.

These wooden pots were made for storing salves. They were found on the Mary Rose.

saw: (see AMPUTATION)

scalpel: sharp knife used by doctors in *operations*, strong enough to cut skin and muscle, but not bone. Tudor scalpels look very similar to modern scalpels. In Tudor times, the use of unclean scalpels caused *infection*, which led to more illness.

19

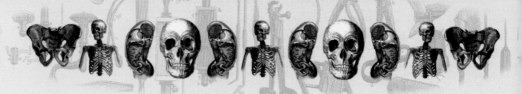

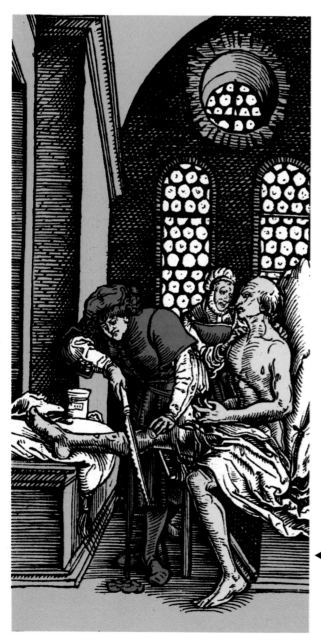

surgeon: person who performs *surgery*. (see SURGERY and OPERATION)

surgery: to cut people open in *operations* to try and cure them. Surgery in Tudor times was very different from today. No proper *anaesthetics* were used, so it was very painful. *Amputations* were the most common type of surgery. Tudor patients often died in surgery, due to severe pain, or blood loss. Sometimes patients died later because they were *infected* by dirty *instruments*. (see AMPUTATION)

toothache: (see DENTIST)

unhygienic: opposite of hygienic. (see HYGIENE)

◀ A drawing of an amputation from 1535. The barber-surgeon's room looks very different from a modern operating theatre.

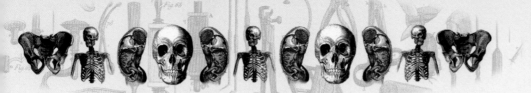
Vesalius, Andreas (1516–1564): famous

Tudor doctor. Vesalius learned about the human body by *dissection* and wrote many books about *anatomy*. He made medical students watch dissections. Now all medical students watch and perform dissections to learn about the human body. (SEE ANATOMY and DISSECTION)

wart: small hard lump on the

skin. Tudor doctors had many strange cures for warts, like putting a dead mouse on the wart, then burying the mouse. Another was to give money to an old woman, so that she would wish the wart away.

Andreas Vesalius, ➤ drawn in 1542.

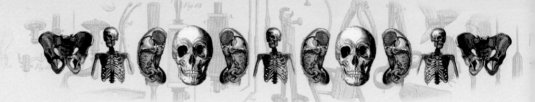

wound man: picture of a man with many cuts
and injuries, with information on how to treat them. All
Tudor doctors and *surgeons* had a wound man. It showed
what to do when a patient came with a
wound from battle, e.g.
for a cut from a spear, put
a red-hot poker in it to
stop the bleeding.

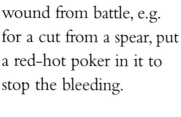

This wound man
was drawn in the
16th century. It
would have also had
information on it,
telling the doctor
how to treat each of
these injuries.

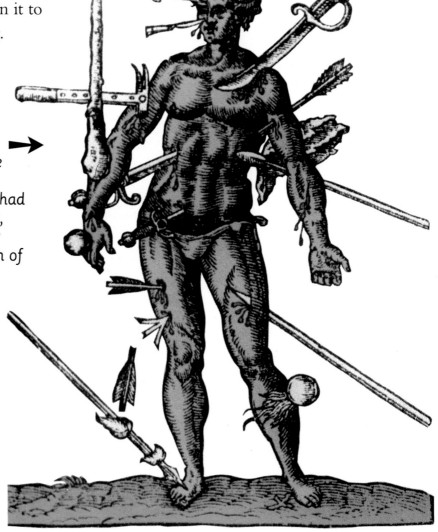

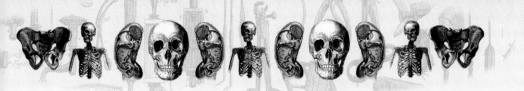

Head
Aries, the ram

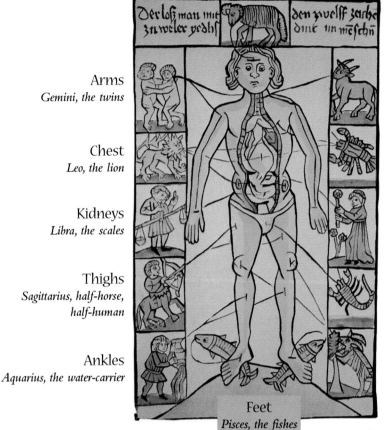

Arms
Gemini, the twins

Chest
Leo, the lion

Kidneys
Libra, the scales

Thighs
*Sagittarius, half-horse,
half-human*

Ankles
Aquarius, the water-carrier

Ears, nose and throat
Taurus, the bull

Stomach
Cancer, the crab

Bladder
Virgo, the virgin

Groin
Scorpio, the scorpion

Knees
Capricorn, the goat

Feet
Pisces, the fishes

zodiac:

Twelve different patterns of stars in the sky, each with
a name and a creature connected to a particular time
of the year. Tudor doctors believed that the signs of the
zodiac affected parts of the body. They thought that
cures would be more successful if the affected part of
the body was treated during its zodiac time.

*The zodiac signs,
and the parts of
the body they
ruled. The picture
in the centre is
from a Tudor book
of medicine.*

Index